HAL•LEONARD

BLUES PLAY-ALONG

Book & Audio for B♭, E♭, Bass Clef and C instruments

VOLUME 1

CHICAGO BLUES

PLAY 8 SONGS WITH A PROFESSIONAL BAND

T0039920

HOW TO USE THE AUDIO:

Each song has multiple tracks:

1) Full Stereo Mix

All recorded instruments are present on this track.

2) Minus Guitar & Harmonica Mix

3) Minus Piano & Bass Mix

4) Split Track to Adjust Balance

PLAYBACK+

Speed • Pitch • Balance • Loop

To access audio visit:
www.halleonard.com/mylibrary

Enter Code
6940-7451-5837-6839

ISBN 978-1-4234-5347-5

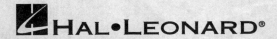

Hal•Leonard®

Visit Hal Leonard Online at
www.halleonard.com

Contact us:
Hal Leonard
7777 West Bluemound Road
Milwaukee, WI 53213
Email: info@halleonard.com

In Europe, contact:
Hal Leonard Europe Limited
42 Wigmore Street
Marylebone, London, W1U 2RN
Email: info@halleonardeurope.com

In Australia, contact:
Hal Leonard Australia Pty. Ltd.
4 Lentara Court
Cheltenham, Victoria, 3192 Australia
Email: info@halleonard.com.au

CHICAGO BLUES

All Your Love
(I Miss Loving)

C Version

Words and Music by Otis Rush

ADDITIONAL LYRICS

2. All the love, pretty baby,
   I have in store for you.
   All the love, pretty baby,
   I have in store for you.
   The way I love you, baby,
   I know you love me, too.

Easy Baby

Written by Willie Dixon

C Version

ADDITIONAL LYRICS

2. Now you don't have to treat me right.
   Just kiss me baby, now hold me tight.

3. Now you don't have to treat me right.
   Just kiss me baby, now hold me light.

I Ain't Got You

By Calvin Carter

C Version

8

Additional Lyrics

2. I got a closet full of clothes.
Don't matter where I go.
You keep a ring in my nose,
But I ain't got you.

I'm Your
Hoochie Coochie Man

Written by Willie Dixon

C Version

WELL,__ YOU KNOW I'M THE HOO - CHIE COO - CHIE MAN.__

EV - 'RY - BOD - Y __ KNOWS I'M HERE.__

GUITAR SOLO

THE WHOLE __ ROUND WORLD KNOWS I'M HERE.

ADDITIONAL LYRICS

2. I GOT A BLACK CAT BONE,
I GOT A MOJO TOO.
I GOT THE JOHN THE CONQUERROOT,
I'M GONNA MESS WITH YOU.
I'M GONNA MAKE YOU GIRLS
LEAD ME BY MY HAND.
THEN THE WORLD'LL KNOW
I'M THE HOOCHIE COOCHIE MAN.

3. ON THE SEVENTH HOUR,
ON THE SEVENTH DAY,
ON THE SEVENTH MONTH,
THE SEVENTH DOCTOR SAY,
"YOU WERE BORN FOR GOOD LUCK,
AND THAT YOU'LL SEE."
I GOT SEVEN HUNDRED DOLLARS,
DON'T YOU MESS WITH ME.

Killing Floor

Words and Music by Chester Burnett

C Version

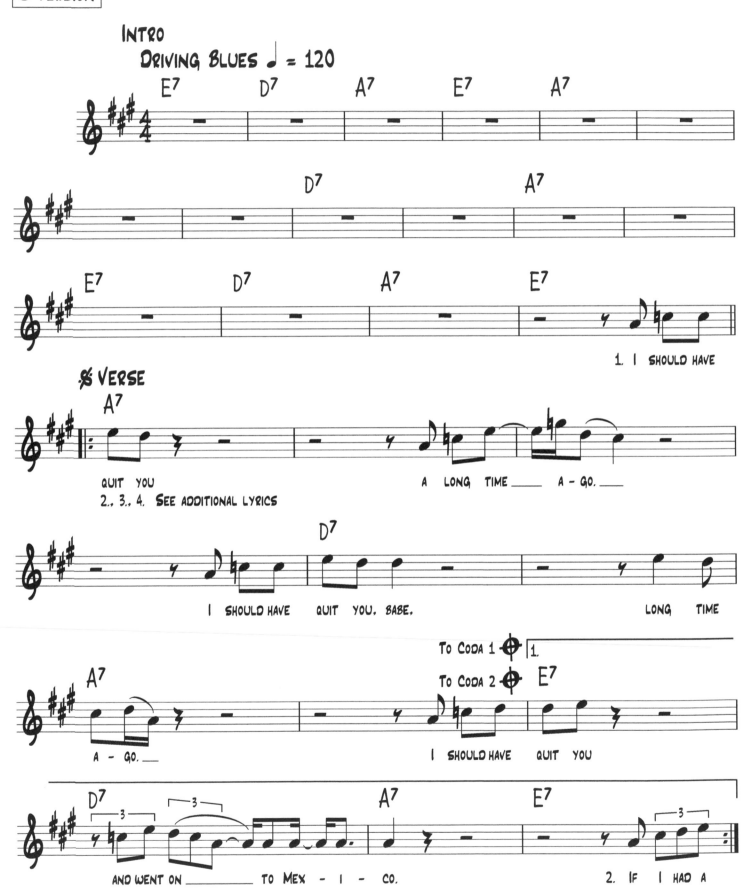

D.S. AL CODA 1
D.S. AL CODA 2
D.S.S. AND FADE

Additional Lyrics

2. If I had a followed my first mind,
   If I had a followed my first mind,
   I'd a been gone since my second time.

3. I should have went on when my friend come from Mexico at me.
   I should have went on when my friend come from Mexico at me.
   But now I'm foolin' with you, baby, I let you put me on the killing floor.

4. God knows I should have been gone.
   God knows I should have been gone.
   Then I wouldn't have been here, down on the killing floor.

Mary Had a Little Lamb

Written by Buddy Guy

C Version

1. Mar-y had a lit-tle lamb. _____

2. See additional lyrics

Its fleece was white as snow, yeah. _ Ev-'ry-where the child

went. The lamb. _ The lamb was sure to go, yeah.

2. He fol-lowed her to school _

Additional Lyrics

2. He followed her to school one day
   And broke the teacher's rule.
   And what a time did they have
   That day at school.

4. No, no, no, no, no, no, oo.
   No, no, no, no, yeah.
   No, no, no, no, no, yeah.
   No, no, no, no, no, no, yeah.
   Uh, uh, uh, uh. Hit it.

Messin' with the Kid

Words and Music by Mel London

C Version

INTRO
UPTEMPO BLUES ♩ = 142
N.C.

1. A

%. VERSE
C7

WHAT THIS I HEAR-IN' GO-IN' ALL A-ROUND TOWN? THE
2., 3., 4. See additional lyrics

PEO- PLE ARE SAY - IN' YOU'RE GON - NA PUT THE KID A YEAH,

F7

DOWN. YEAH, LOOK AT WHAT YOU DID.

G7   F7   4TH TIME, TO CODA ⊕

YOU CAN CALL ___ IT WHAT YOU WANT. I ___ CALL IT MESS-IN' WITH THE

ADDITIONAL LYRICS

2. You know the kid's no child, and I don't play. I says what I mean, I mean what I say.
But oh, yeah, yeah, yeah, yeah. Oh, look at what you did.
You can call it what you want, I call it messin' with the kid. Hey, look a here.

3. You can tell me you love me, you tell me a lie, but I love you baby till I die.
But oh, no. Oh, look at what you did.
You can call it what you want, I call it messin' with the kid.

4. We're gonna take the kid's car and drive around town, and tell ev'rybody you're, Lord, puttin' him down.
But oh, yeah, yeah, yeah, yeah. Oh, look at what you did.
You can call it what you want, I call it messin' with the...

Sweet Home Chicago

Words and Music by Robert Johnson

C Version

BACK __ TO THAT SAME OLD PLACE.

SWEET HOME __ CHI - CA - GO? _____

TO CODA 2

D.S. AL CODA 1

4. COME

CODA 1

GUITAR SOLO

2ND TIME, D.S.S. AL CODA 2

CODA 2

6. AH, COME ON. __

VERSE

BA - BY, DON'T YOU __ WAN - NA GO? _____

COME ON, _____ BA - BY, DON'T YOU WAN - NA GO __

BACK __ TO THAT SAME OLD __ PLACE, __

SWEET HOME __ CHI - CA - GO? _____

19

All Your Love
(I Miss Loving)
Words and Music by Otis Rush

B♭ Version

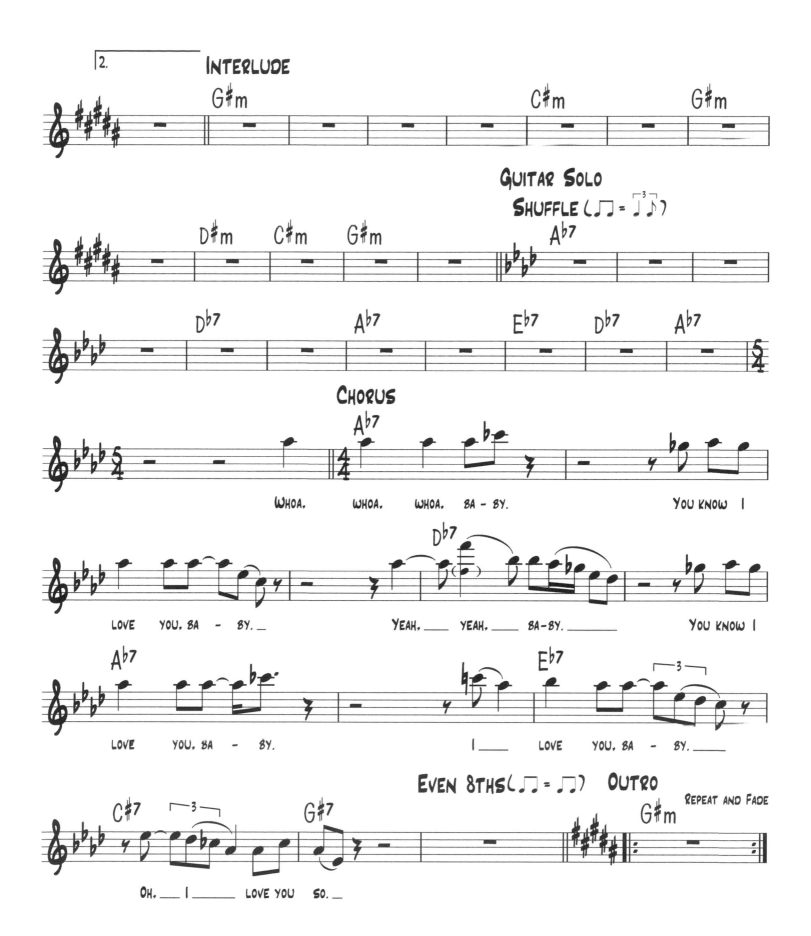

ADDITIONAL LYRICS

2. All the love, pretty baby,
   I have in store for you.
   All the love, pretty baby,
   I have in store for you.
   The way I love you, baby,
   I know you love me, too.

Easy Baby

Written by Willie Dixon

ADDITIONAL LYRICS

2. Now you don't have to treat me right.
   Just kiss me baby, now hold me tight.

3. Now you don't have to treat me right.
   Just kiss me baby, now hold me light.

I Ain't Got You

By Calvin Carter

Bb Version

Additional Lyrics

2. I got a closet full of clothes.
   Don't matter where I go.
   You keep a ring in my nose.
   But I ain't got you.

I'm Your Hoochie Coochie Man

Written by Willie Dixon

Bb Version

WELL,— YOU KNOW I'M THE HOO - CHIE COO - CHIE MAN,—

EV - 'RY - BOD - Y ___ KNOWS I'M HERE.—

GUITAR SOLO

THE WHOLE ___ ROUND WORLD KNOWS I'M HERE.

ADDITIONAL LYRICS

2. I got a black cat bone,
   I got a mojo too.
   I got the John the Conquerroot,
   I'm gonna mess with you.
   I'm gonna make you girls
   Lead me by my hand.
   Then the world'll know
   I'm the Hoochie Coochie man.

3. On the seventh hour,
   On the seventh day,
   On the seventh month,
   The seventh doctor say,
   "You were born for good luck.
   And that you'll see."
   I got seven hundred dollars,
   Don't you mess with me.

Killing Floor

Words and Music by Chester Burnett

B♭ Version

Additional Lyrics

2. If I had a followed my first mind,
   If I had a followed my first mind,
   I'd a been gone since my second time.

3. I should have went on when my friend come from Mexico at me.
   I should have went on when my friend come from Mexico at me.
   But now I'm foolin' with you, baby, I let you put me on the killing floor.

4. God knows I should have been gone.
   God knows I should have been gone.
   Then I wouldn't have been here, down on the killing floor.

Mary Had a Little Lamb

Written by Buddy Guy

Bb Version

Additional Lyrics

2. He followed her to school one day
   And broke the teacher's rule.
   And what a time did they have
   That day at school.

4. No, no, no, no, no, no, oo.
   No, no, no, no, yeah.
   No, no, no, no, no, yeah.
   No, no, no, no, no, no, yeah.
   Uh, uh, uh, uh. Hit it.

Messin' with the Kid

Words and Music by Mel London

Bb Version

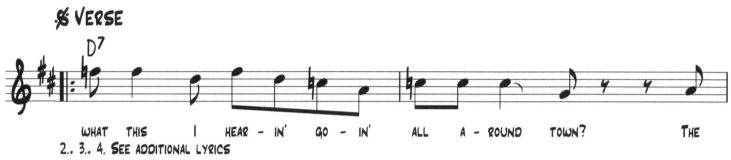

Additional Lyrics

2. You know the kid's no child, and I don't play. I says what I mean, I mean what I say.
   But oh, yeah, yeah, yeah, yeah. Oh, look at what you did.
   You can call it what you want, I call it messin' with the kid. Hey, look a here.

3. You can tell me you love me, you tell me a lie, but I love you baby till I die.
   But oh, no. Oh, look at what you did.
   You can call it what you want, I call it messin' with the kid.

4. We're gonna take the kid's car and drive around town, and tell ev'rybody you're, Lord, puttin' him down.
   But oh, yeah, yeah, yeah, yeah. Oh, look at what you did.
   You can call it what you want, I call it messin' with the...

Sweet Home Chicago

Words and Music by Robert Johnson

All Your Love
(I Miss Loving)

Words and Music by Otis Rush

Eb Version

Interlude

Guitar Solo
Shuffle (♫ = ⌐³⌐ ♪♪)

Chorus

Whoa, whoa, whoa, ba-by. You know I

love you, ba - by. ___ Yeah, ___ yeah, ___ ba-by. ___ You know I

love you, ba - by. I ___ love you, ba - by. ___

Even 8ths (♫ = ♫) **Outro**
Repeat and Fade

Oh, ___ I ___ love you so. ___

Additional Lyrics

2. All the love, pretty baby,
   I have in store for you.
   All the love, pretty baby,
   I have in store for you.
   The way I love you, baby,
   I know you love me, too.

Easy Baby

Written by Willie Dixon

Eb Version

I Ain't Got You

By Calvin Carter

Eb Version

ADDITIONAL LYRICS

2. I GOT A CLOSET FULL OF CLOTHES.
    DON'T MATTER WHERE I GO.
    YOU KEEP A RING IN MY NOSE,
    BUT I AIN'T GOT YOU.

I'm Your Hoochie Coochie Man

Written by Willie Dixon

E♭ Version

WELL,__ YOU KNOW I'M THE HOO - CHIE COO - CHIE MAN, __

EV - 'RY - BOD - Y ____ KNOWS I'M HERE. __

GUITAR SOLO

THE WHOLE __ ROUND WORLD KNOWS I'M HERE.

Additional Lyrics

2. I got a black cat bone,
   I got a mojo too.
   I got the John the Conquerroot,
   I'm gonna mess with you.
   I'm gonna make you girls
   Lead me by my hand.
   Then the world'll know
   I'm the Hoochie Coochie man.

3. On the seventh hour,
   On the seventh day,
   On the seventh month,
   The seventh doctor say,
   "You were born for good luck,
   And that you'll see."
   I got seven hundred dollars,
   Don't you mess with me.

Killing Floor

Words and Music by Chester Burnett

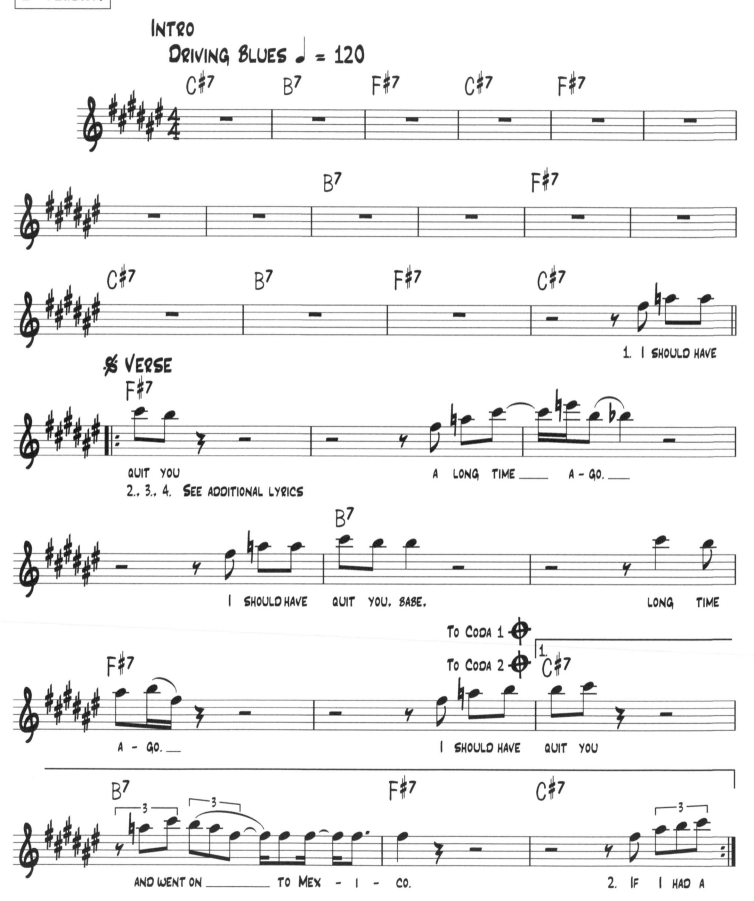

GONE

SINCE MY ___ SEC-OND TIME. ___

%.% GUITAR SOLO

D.S. AL CODA 1

3. I SHOULD HAVE

CODA 1

FOOL-IN' WITH YOU, BA - BY, I LET YOU

PUT ME ON THE ___ KILL-ING

D.S. AL CODA 2

FLOOR.

4. GOD KNOWS ___

CODA 2

WOULD-N'T HAVE BEEN HERE.

D.S.S. AND FADE

DOWN _____ ON THE KILL-ING

FLOOR.

YEAH.

ADDITIONAL LYRICS

2. IF I HAD A FOLLOWED MY FIRST MIND,
   IF I HAD A FOLLOWED MY FIRST MIND,
   I'D A BEEN GONE SINCE MY SECOND TIME.

3. I SHOULD HAVE WENT ON WHEN MY FRIEND COME FROM MEXICO AT ME.
   I SHOULD HAVE WENT ON WHEN MY FRIEND COME FROM MEXICO AT ME.
   BUT NOW I'M FOOLIN' WITH YOU, BABY, I LET YOU PUT ME ON THE KILLING FLOOR.

4. GOD KNOWS I SHOULD HAVE BEEN GONE.
   GOD KNOWS I SHOULD HAVE BEEN GONE.
   THEN I WOULDN'T HAVE BEEN HERE, DOWN ON THE KILLING FLOOR.

Mary Had a Little Lamb

Written by Buddy Guy

1. Mar-y had a lit-tle lamb. _____
2. See additional lyrics

Its fleece was white as snow. Yeah. _

Ev-'ry-where the child went.

The lamb. _ The lamb was sure to go. Yeah.

2. He fol-lowed her to school _

ADDITIONAL LYRICS

2. HE FOLLOWED HER TO SCHOOL ONE DAY
   AND BROKE THE TEACHER'S RULE.
   AND WHAT A TIME DID THEY HAVE
   THAT DAY AT SCHOOL.

4. NO, NO, NO, NO, NO, NO, OO.
   NO, NO, NO, NO, YEAH.
   NO, NO, NO, NO, NO, YEAH.
   NO, NO, NO, NO, NO, NO, YEAH.
   UH, UH, UH, UH. HIT IT.

Messin' with the Kid

Words and Music by Mel London

Eb Version

Additional Lyrics

2. You know the kid's no child, and I don't play. I says what I mean, I mean what I say.
   But oh, yeah, yeah, yeah, yeah. Oh, look at what you did.
   You can call it what you want, I call it messin' with the kid. Hey, look a here.

3. You can tell me you love me, you tell me a lie, but I love you baby till I die.
   But oh, no. Oh, look at what you did.
   You can call it what you want, I call it messin' with the kid.

4. We're gonna take the kid's car and drive around town, and tell ev'rybody you're, Lord, puttin' him down.
   But oh, yeah, yeah, yeah, yeah. Oh, look at what you did.
   You can call it what you want, I call it messin' with the...

Sweet Home Chicago

Words and Music by Robert Johnson

BACK __ TO THAT SAME OLD __ PLACE. __

SWEET HOME __ CHI - CA - GO? __

To Coda 2   D.S. AL CODA 1

4. COME

Coda 1

GUITAR SOLO

2ND TIME, D.S.S. AL CODA 2   Coda 2

6. AH, COME ON, __

VERSE

BA - BY, DON'T YOU __ WAN - NA GO? __

COME ON, __   BA - BY, DON'T YOU WAN - NA GO __

BACK __ TO THAT SAME OLD __ PLACE, __

SWEET HOME __ CHI - CA - GO? __

51

All Your Love
(I Miss Loving)

Words and Music by Otis Rush

ADDITIONAL LYRICS

2. ALL THE LOVE, PRETTY BABY,
   I HAVE IN STORE FOR YOU.
   ALL THE LOVE, PRETTY BABY,
   I HAVE IN STORE FOR YOU.
   THE WAY I LOVE YOU, BABY,
   I KNOW YOU LOVE ME, TOO.

Easy Baby

Written by Willie Dixon

Additional Lyrics

2. Now you don't have to treat me right.
   Just kiss me baby, now hold me tight.

3. Now you don't have to treat me right.
   Just kiss me baby, now hold me light.

I Ain't Got You

By Calvin Carter

Additional Lyrics

2. I got a closet full of clothes.
    Don't matter where I go.
    You keep a ring in my nose,
    But I ain't got you.

I'm Your
Hoochie Coochie Man

C Version

Written by Willie Dixon

Intro

Slow Shuffle ♩. = 75

Verse

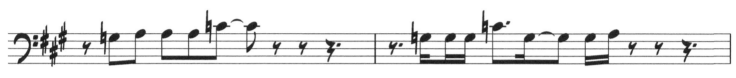

1. The gyp-sy wom-an told my moth-er
2., 3. See additional lyrics

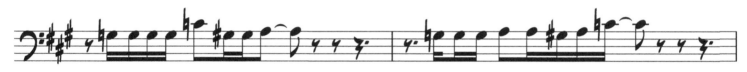

be-fore I was born. __   "You got a boy childs __ com-in'

gon na be a son-of-a-gun. __   He gon na make pret-ty wom-ens __

jump an' shout. __   Then the world wan-na know

Chorus

D7

what this all a-bout?" __   But you know I'm here. ____

A7

Ev-'ry-bod-y knows __ I'm here. ____

WELL,_ YOU KNOW I'M THE HOO - CHIE COO - CHIE MAN,_

EV - 'RY - BOD - Y _ KNOWS I'M HERE._

GUITAR SOLO

THE WHOLE _ ROUND WORLD KNOWS I'M HERE.

ADDITIONAL LYRICS

2. I GOT A BLACK CAT BONE,
   I GOT A MOJO TOO.
   I GOT THE JOHN THE CONQUERROOT,
   I'M GONNA MESS WITH YOU.
   I'M GONNA MAKE YOU GIRLS
   LEAD ME BY MY HAND.
   THEN THE WORLD'LL KNOW
   I'M THE HOOCHIE COOCHIE MAN.

3. ON THE SEVENTH HOUR,
   ON THE SEVENTH DAY,
   ON THE SEVENTH MONTH,
   THE SEVENTH DOCTOR SAY,
   "YOU WERE BORN FOR GOOD LUCK,
   AND THAT YOU'LL SEE."
   I GOT SEVEN HUNDRED DOLLARS,
   DON'T YOU MESS WITH ME.

Killing Floor

Words and Music by Chester Burnett

Additional Lyrics

2. If I had a followed my first mind,
   If I had a followed my first mind,
   I'd a been gone since my second time.

3. I should have went on when my friend come from Mexico at me.
   I should have went on when my friend come from Mexico at me.
   But now I'm foolin' with you, baby, I let you put me on the killing floor.

4. God knows I should have been gone.
   God knows I should have been gone.
   Then I wouldn't have been here, down on the killing floor.

Mary Had a Little Lamb

Written by Buddy Guy

Additional Lyrics

2. He followed her to school one day
   And broke the teacher's rule.
   And what a time did they have
   That day at school.

4. No, no, no, no, no, no, oo.
   No, no, no, no, yeah.
   No, no, no, no, no, yeah.
   No, no, no, no, no, no, yeah.
   Uh, uh, uh, uh. Hit it.

Messin' with the Kid

Words and Music by Mel London

ADDITIONAL LYRICS

ADDITIONAL LYRICS

2. YOU KNOW THE KID'S NO CHILD, AND I DON'T PLAY. I SAYS WHAT I MEAN, I MEAN WHAT I SAY.
   BUT OH, YEAH, YEAH, YEAH, YEAH. OH, LOOK AT WHAT YOU DID.
   YOU CAN CALL IT WHAT YOU WANT, I CALL IT MESSIN' WITH THE KID. HEY, LOOK A HERE.

3. YOU CAN TELL ME YOU LOVE ME, YOU TELL ME A LIE, BUT I LOVE YOU BABY TILL I DIE.
   BUT OH, NO. OH, LOOK AT WHAT YOU DID.
   YOU CAN CALL IT WHAT YOU WANT, I CALL IT MESSIN' WITH THE KID.

4. WE'RE GONNA TAKE THE KID'S CAR AND DRIVE AROUND TOWN, AND TELL EV'RYBODY YOU'RE, LORD, PUTTIN' HIM DOWN.
   BUT OH, YEAH, YEAH, YEAH, YEAH. OH, LOOK AT WHAT YOU DID.
   YOU CAN CALL IT WHAT YOU WANT, I CALL IT MESSIN' WITH THE...

Sweet Home Chicago

Words and Music by Robert Johnson

BACK ___ TO THAT SAME OLD ___ PLACE, _

SWEET HOME ___ CHI - CA - GO? ___

To Coda 2 ⊕   D.S. AL CODA 1

4. COME

⊕ CODA 1

GUITAR SOLO

2ND TIME, D.S.S. AL CODA 2   ⊕ CODA 2

6. AH, COME ON, ___

VERSE

BA - BY, DON'T YOU ___ WAN - NA GO? ___

COME ON, ___   BA - BY, DON'T YOU WAN - NA GO _

BACK ___ TO THAT SAME OLD ___ PLACE, _

SWEET HOME ___ CHI - CA - GO? ___

For use with all B-flat, E-flat, Bass Clef and C instruments, the Jazz Play-Along® Series is the ultimate learning tool for all jazz musicians. With musician-friendly lead sheets, melody cues, and other split-track audio choices included, these first-of-a-kind packages help you master improvisation while playing some of the greatest tunes of all time. FOR STUDY, each tune includes a split track with: melody cue with proper style and inflection • professional rhythm tracks • choruses for soloing • removable bass part • removable piano part. FOR PERFORMANCE, each tune also has: an additional full stereo accompaniment track (no melody) • additional choruses for soloing.

1A. MAIDEN VOYAGE/ALL BLUES
00843158 .... $22.99

1. DUKE ELLINGTON
00841644 .... $16.99

2. MILES DAVIS
00841645 .... $17.99

3. THE BLUES
00841646 .... $19.99

4. JAZZ BALLADS
00841691 .... $17.99

5. BEST OF BEBOP
00841689 .... $17.99

6. JAZZ CLASSICS WITH EASY CHANGES
00841690 .... $16.99

7. ESSENTIAL JAZZ STANDARDS
00843000 .... $17.99

8. ANTONIO CARLOS JOBIM AND THE ART OF THE BOSSA NOVA
00843001 .... $16.99

9. DIZZY GILLESPIE
00843002 .... $19.99

10. DISNEY CLASSICS
00843003 .... $16.99

12. ESSENTIAL JAZZ CLASSICS
00843005 .... $16.99

13. JOHN COLTRANE
00843006 .... $17.99

14. IRVING BERLIN
00843007 .... $16.99

15. RODGERS & HAMMERSTEIN
00843008 .... $16.99

16. COLE PORTER
00843009 .... $17.99

17. COUNT BASIE
00843010 .... $17.99

18. HAROLD ARLEN
00843011 .... $17.99

20. CHRISTMAS CAROLS
00843080 .... $16.99

21. RODGERS AND HART CLASSICS
00843014 .... $16.99

22. WAYNE SHORTER
00843015 .... $17.99

23. LATIN JAZZ
00843016 .... $19.99

24. EARLY JAZZ STANDARDS
00843017 .... $16.99

25. CHRISTMAS JAZZ
00843018 .... $17.99

26. CHARLIE PARKER
00843019 .... $16.99

27. GREAT JAZZ STANDARDS
00843020 .... $17.99

28. BIG BAND ERA
00843021 .... $17.99

29. LENNON AND MCCARTNEY
00843022 .... $24.99

30. BLUES' BEST
00843023 .... $16.99

31. JAZZ IN THREE
00843024 .... $16.99

32. BEST OF SWING
00843025 .... $17.99

33. SONNY ROLLINS
00843029 .... $16.99

34. ALL TIME STANDARDS
00843030 .... $17.99

35. BLUESY JAZZ
00843031 .... $17.99

36. HORACE SILVER
00843032 .... $19.99

37. BILL EVANS
00843033 .... $16.99

38. YULETIDE JAZZ
00843034 .... $16.99

39. "ALL THE THINGS YOU ARE" & MORE JEROME KERN SONGS
00843035 .... $19.99

40. BOSSA NOVA
00843036 .... $19.99

41. CLASSIC DUKE ELLINGTON
00843037 .... $16.99

42. GERRY MULLIGAN FAVORITES
00843038 .... $16.99

43. GERRY MULLIGAN CLASSICS
00843039 .... $19.99

45. GEORGE GERSHWIN
00103643 .... $24.99

47. CLASSIC JAZZ BALLADS
00843043 .... $17.99

48. BEBOP CLASSICS
00843044 .... $16.99

49. MILES DAVIS STANDARDS
00843045 .... $19.99

52. STEVIE WONDER
00843048 .... $17.99

53. RHYTHM CHANGES
00843049 .... $16.99

55. BENNY GOLSON
00843052 .... $19.99

56. "GEORGIA ON MY MIND" & OTHER SONGS BY HOAGY CARMICHAEL
00843056 .... $17.99

57. VINCE GUARALDI
00843057 .... $16.99

58. MORE LENNON AND MCCARTNEY
00843059 .... $17.99

59. SOUL JAZZ
00843060 .... $17.99

60. DEXTER GORDON
00843061 .... $16.99

61. MONGO SANTAMARIA
00843062 .... $16.99

62. JAZZ-ROCK FUSION
00843063 .... $19.99

63. CLASSICAL JAZZ
00843064 .... $16.99

64. TV TUNES
00843065 .... $16.99

65. SMOOTH JAZZ
00843066 .... $19.99

66. A CHARLIE BROWN CHRISTMAS
00843067 .... $16.99

67. CHICK COREA
00843068 .... $22.99

68. CHARLES MINGUS
00843069 .... $19.99

71. COLE PORTER CLASSICS
00843073 .... $16.99

72. CLASSIC JAZZ BALLADS
00843074 .... $16.99

73. JAZZ/BLUES
00843075 .... $16.99

74. BEST JAZZ CLASSICS
00843076 .... $16.99

75. PAUL DESMOND
00843077 .... $17.99

78. STEELY DAN
00843070 .... $19.99

79. MILES DAVIS CLASSICS
00843081 .... $16.99

80. JIMI HENDRIX
00843083 .... $17.99

83. ANDREW LLOYD WEBBER
00843104 .... $16.99

84. BOSSA NOVA CLASSICS
00843105 .... $17.99

85. MOTOWN HITS
00843109 .... $17.99

86. BENNY GOODMAN
00843110 .... $17.99

87. DIXIELAND
00843111 .... $16.99

90. **THELONIOUS MONK CLASSICS**
   00841262 .... $16.99

91. **THELONIOUS MONK FAVORITES**
   00841263 .... $17.99

92. **LEONARD BERNSTEIN**
   00450134 .... $16.99

93. **DISNEY FAVORITES**
   00843142 .... $16.99

94. **RAY**
   00843143 .... $19.99

95. **JAZZ AT THE LOUNGE**
   00843144 .... $17.99

96. **LATIN JAZZ STANDARDS**
   00843145 .... $16.99

97. **MAYBE I'M AMAZED***
   00843148 .... $16.99

98. **DAVE FRISHBERG**
   00843149 .... $16.99

99. **SWINGING STANDARDS**
   00843150 .... $16.99

100. **LOUIS ARMSTRONG**
   00740423 .... $19.99

101. **BUD POWELL**
   00843152 .... $16.99

102. **JAZZ POP**
   00843153 .... $19.99

103. **ON GREEN DOLPHIN STREET
   & OTHER JAZZ CLASSICS**
   00843154 .... $16.99

104. **ELTON JOHN**
   00843155 .... $19.99

105. **SOULFUL JAZZ**
   00843151 .... $17.99

106. **SLO' JAZZ**
   00843117 .... $16.99

107. **MOTOWN CLASSICS**
   00843116 .... $17.99

108. **JAZZ WALTZ**
   00843159 .... $16.99

109. **OSCAR PETERSON**
   00843160 .... $16.99

110. **JUST STANDARDS**
   00843161 .... $16.99

111. **COOL CHRISTMAS**
   00843162 .... $16.99

112. **PAQUITO D'RIVERA – LATIN JAZZ***
   48020662 .... $16.99

113. **PAQUITO D'RIVERA – BRAZILIAN JAZZ***
   48020663 .... $19.99

114. **MODERN JAZZ QUARTET FAVORITES**
   00843163 .... $16.99

115. **THE SOUND OF MUSIC**
   00843164 .... $16.99

116. **JACO PASTORIUS**
   00843165 .... $17.99

117. **ANTONIO CARLOS JOBIM – MORE HITS**
   00843166 .... $17.99

118. **BIG JAZZ STANDARDS COLLECTION**
   00843167 .... $27.50

119. **JELLY ROLL MORTON**
   00843168 .... $16.99

120. **J.S. BACH**
   00843169 .... $17.99

121. **DJANGO REINHARDT**
   00843170 .... $16.99

122. **PAUL SIMON**
   00843182 .... $16.99

123. **BACHARACH & DAVID**
   00843185 .... $16.99

124. **JAZZ-ROCK HORN HITS**
   00843186 .... $16.99

125. **SAMMY NESTICO**
   00843187 .... $16.99

126. **COUNT BASIE CLASSICS**
   00843157 .... $16.99

127. **CHUCK MANGIONE**
   00843188 .... $19.99

128. **VOCAL STANDARDS (LOW VOICE)**
   00843189 .... $16.99

129. **VOCAL STANDARDS (HIGH VOICE)**
   00843190 .... $16.99

130. **VOCAL JAZZ (LOW VOICE)**
   00843191 .... $16.99

131. **VOCAL JAZZ (HIGH VOICE)**
   00843192 .... $16.99

132. **STAN GETZ ESSENTIALS**
   00843193 .... $17.99

133. **STAN GETZ FAVORITES**
   00843194 .... $16.99

134. **NURSERY RHYMES***
   00843196 .... $17.99

135. **JEFF BECK**
   00843197 .... $16.99

136. **NAT ADDERLEY**
   00843198 .... $16.99

137. **WES MONTGOMERY**
   00843199 .... $16.99

138. **FREDDIE HUBBARD**
   00843200 .... $16.99

139. **JULIAN "CANNONBALL" ADDERLEY**
   00843201 .... $16.99

140. **JOE ZAWINUL**
   00843202 .... $16.99

141. **BILL EVANS STANDARDS**
   00843156 .... $16.99

142. **CHARLIE PARKER GEMS**
   00843222 .... $16.99

143. **JUST THE BLUES**
   00843223 .... $16.99

144. **LEE MORGAN**
   00843229 .... $16.99

145. **COUNTRY STANDARDS**
   00843230 .... $16.99

146. **RAMSEY LEWIS**
   00843231 .... $16.99

147. **SAMBA**
   00843232 .... $16.99

148. **JOHN COLTRANE FAVORITES**
   00843233 .... $16.99

149. **JOHN COLTRANE – GIANT STEPS**
   00843234 .... $16.99

150. **JAZZ IMPROV BASICS**
   00843195 .... $19.99

151. **MODERN JAZZ QUARTET CLASSICS**
   00843209 .... $16.99

152. **J.J. JOHNSON**
   00843210 .... $16.99

153. **KENNY GARRETT**
   00843212 .... $16.99

154. **HENRY MANCINI**
   00843213 .... $17.99

155. **SMOOTH JAZZ CLASSICS**
   00843215 .... $17.99

156. **THELONIOUS MONK – EARLY GEMS**
   00843216 .... $16.99

157. **HYMNS**
   00843217 .... $16.99

158. **JAZZ COVERS ROCK**
   00843219 .... $16.99

159. **MOZART**
   00843220 .... $16.99

160. **GEORGE SHEARING**
   14041531 .... $16.99

161. **DAVE BRUBECK**
   14041556 .... $16.99

162. **BIG CHRISTMAS COLLECTION**
   00843221 .... $24.99

163. **JOHN COLTRANE STANDARDS**
   00843235 .... $16.99

164. **HERB ALPERT**
   14041775 .... $19.99

165. **GEORGE BENSON**
   00843240 .... $17.99

166. **ORNETTE COLEMAN**
   00843241 .... $16.99

167. **JOHNNY MANDEL**
   00103642 .... $16.99

168. **TADD DAMERON**
   00103663 .... $16.99

169. **BEST JAZZ STANDARDS**
   00109249 .... $24.99

170. **ULTIMATE JAZZ STANDARDS**
   00109250 .... $24.99

171. **RADIOHEAD**
   00109305 .... $16.99

172. **POP STANDARDS**
   00111669 .... $16.99

174. **TIN PAN ALLEY**
   00119125 .... $16.99

175. **TANGO**
   00119836 .... $16.99

176. **JOHNNY MERCER**
   00119838 .... $16.99

177. **THE II-V-I PROGRESSION**
   00843239 .... $24.99

178. **JAZZ/FUNK**
   00121902 .... $17.99

179. **MODAL JAZZ**
   00122273 .... $16.99

180. **MICHAEL JACKSON**
   00122327 .... $17.99

181. **BILLY JOEL**
   00122329 .... $19.99

182. **"RHAPSODY IN BLUE" & 7 OTHER
   CLASSICAL-BASED JAZZ PIECES**
   00116847 .... $16.99

183. **SONDHEIM**
   00126253 .... $16.99

184. **JIMMY SMITH**
   00126943 .... $17.99

185. **JAZZ FUSION**
   00127558 .... $17.99

186. **JOE PASS**
   00128391 .... $16.99

187. **CHRISTMAS FAVORITES**
   00128393 .... $16.99

188. **PIAZZOLLA – 10 FAVORITE TUNES**
   48023253 .... $16.99

189. **JOHN LENNON**
   00138678 .... $16.99

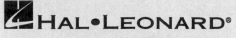
***** These do not include split tracks.

HAL•LEONARD

BLUES PLAY-ALONG

For use with all the C, B♭, Bass Clef and E♭ Instruments, the Hal Leonard Blues Play-Along Series is the ultimate jamming tool for all blues musicians.

With easy-to-read lead sheets, and other split-track choices, these first-of-a-kind packages will bring your local blues jam right into your house! Each song includes two tracks: a full stereo mix, and a split track mix with removable guitar, bass, piano, and harp parts. The CD is playable on any CD player, and is also enhanced so Mac and PC users can adjust the recording to any tempo without changing the pitch!

1. Chicago Blues
All Your Love (I Miss Loving) • Easy Baby • I Ain't Got You • I'm Your Hoochie Coochie Man • Killing Floor • Mary Had a Little Lamb • Messin' with the Kid • Sweet Home Chicago.
00843106 Book/CD Pack $17.99

2. Texas Blues
Hide Away • If You Love Me Like You Say • Mojo Hand • Okie Dokie Stomp • Pride and Joy • Reconsider Baby • T-Bone Shuffle • The Things That I Used to Do.
00843107 Book/CD Pack $12.99

3. Slow Blues
Don't Throw Your Love on Me So Strong • Five Long Years • I Can't Quit You Baby • I Just Want to Make Love to You • The Sky Is Crying • (They Call It) Stormy Monday (Stormy Monday Blues) • Sweet Little Angel • Texas Flood.
00843108 Book/CD Pack $12.99

4. Shuffle Blues
Beautician Blues • Bright Lights, Big City • Further on up the Road • I'm Tore Down • Juke • Let Me Love You Baby • Look at Little Sister • Rock Me Baby.
00843171 Book/CD Pack $12.99

5. B.B. King
Everyday I Have the Blues • It's My Own Fault Darlin' • Just Like a Woman • Please Accept My Love • Sweet Sixteen • The Thrill Is Gone • Why I Sing the Blues • You Upset Me Baby.
00843172 Book/CD Pack $14.99

7. Howlin' Wolf
Built for Comfort • Forty-Four • How Many More Years • Killing Floor • Moanin' at Midnight • Shake for Me • Sitting on Top of the World • Smokestack Lightning.
00843176 Book/CD Pack $12.99

8. Blues Classics
Baby, Please Don't Go • Boom Boom • Born Under a Bad Sign • Dust My Broom • How Long, How Long Blues • I Ain't Superstitious • It Hurts Me Too • My Babe.
00843177 Book/CD Pack $12.99

9. Albert Collins
Brick • Collins' Mix • Don't Lose Your Cool • Frost Bite • Frosty • I Ain't Drunk • Master Charge • Trash Talkin'.
00843178 Book/CD Pack $12.99

10. Uptempo Blues
Cross Road Blues (Crossroads) • Give Me Back My Wig • Got My Mo Jo Working • The House Is Rockin' • Paying the Cost to Be the Boss • Rollin' and Tumblin' • Turn on Your Love Light • You Can't Judge a Book by the Cover.
00843179 Book/CD Pack $12.99

11. Christmas Blues
Back Door Santa • Blue Christmas • Dig That Crazy Santa Claus • Merry Christmas, Baby • Please Come Home for Christmas • Santa Baby • Soulful Christmas.
00843203 Book/CD Pack $12.99

12. Jimmy Reed
Ain't That Lovin' You Baby • Baby, What You Want Me to Do • Big Boss Man • Bright Lights, Big City • Going to New York • Honest I Do • You Don't Have to Go • You Got Me Dizzy.
00843204 Book/CD Pack $12.99

13. Blues Standards
Ain't Nobody's Business • Kansas City • Key to the Highway • Let the Good Times Roll • Night Time Is the Right Time • Route 66 • See See Rider • Stormy Weather (Keeps Rainin' All the Time).
00843205 Book/CD Pack $12.99

14. Muddy Waters
Good Morning Little Schoolgirl • Honey Bee • I Can't Be Satisfied • I'm Ready • Mannish Boy • Rollin' Stone (Catfish Blues) • Trouble No More (Someday Baby) • You Shook Me.
00843206 Book/CD Pack $12.99

15. Blues Ballads
Ain't No Sunshine • As the Years Go Passing By • Darlin' You Know I Love You • Have You Ever Loved a Woman • I'd Rather Go Blind • Somebody Loan Me a Dime • Third Degree • Three Hours past Midnight.
00843207 Book/CD Pack $14.99

17. Stevie Ray Vaughan
Ain't Gone 'n' Give up on Love • Couldn't Stand the Weather • Crossfire • Empty Arms • Honey Bee • Love Struck Baby • Rude Mood • Scuttle Buttin'.
00843214 Book/Audio $14.99

18. Jimi Hendrix
Fire • Foxey Lady • Jam 292 • Little Wing • Red House • Spanish Castle Magic • Voodoo Child (Slight Return) • Who Knows.
00843218 Book/CD Pack $14.99

HAL•LEONARD®

Prices, content, and availability subject to change without notice.   **www.halleonard.com**

The Best-Selling Jazz Book of All Time Is Now Legal!

The Real Books are the most popular jazz books of all time. Since the 1970s, musicians have trusted these volumes to get them through every gig, night after night. The problem is that the books were illegally produced and distributed, without any regard to copyright law, or royalties paid to the composers who created these musical masterpieces.

Hal Leonard is very proud to present the first legitimate and legal editions of these books ever produced. You won't even notice the difference, other than all the notorious errors being fixed: the covers and typeface look the same, the song lists are nearly identical, and the price for our edition is even cheaper than the originals!

Every conscientious musician will appreciate that these books are now produced accurately and ethically, benefitting the songwriters that we owe for some of the greatest tunes of all time!

VOLUME 1
00240221	C Edition	$39.99
00240224	Bb Edition	$39.99
00240225	Eb Edition	$39.99
00240226	Bass Clef Edition	$39.99
00286389	F Edition	$39.99
00240292	C Edition 6 x 9	$35.00
00240339	Bb Edition 6 x 9	$35.00
00147792	Bass Clef Edition 6 x 9	$35.00
00451087	C Edition on CD-ROM	$29.99
00200984	Online Backing Tracks: Selections	$45.00
00110604	Book/USB Flash Drive Backing Tracks Pack	$79.99
00110599	USB Flash Drive Only	$50.00

VOLUME 2
00240222	C Edition	$39.99
00240227	Bb Edition	$39.99
00240228	Eb Edition	$39.99
00240229	Bass Clef Edition	$39.99
00240293	C Edition 6 x 9	$35.00
00125900	Bb Edition 6 x 9	$35.00
00451088	C Edition on CD-ROM	$30.99
00125900	The Real Book – Mini Edition	$35.00
00204126	Backing Tracks on USB Flash Drive	$50.00
00204131	C Edition – USB Flash Drive Pack	$79.99

VOLUME 3
00240233	C Edition	$39.99
00240284	Bb Edition	$39.99
00240285	Eb Edition	$39.99
00240286	Bass Clef Edition	$39.99
00240338	C Edition 6 x 9	$35.00
00451089	C Edition on CD-ROM	$29.99

VOLUME 4
00240296	C Edition	$39.99
00103348	Bb Edition	$39.99
00103349	Eb Edition	$39.99
00103350	Bass Clef Edition	$39.99

VOLUME 5
00240349	C Edition	$39.99
00175278	Bb Edition	$39.99
00175279	Eb Edition	$39.99

VOLUME 6
00240534	C Edition	$39.99
00223637	Eb Edition	$39.99

Also available:
00154230	The Real Bebop Book	$34.99
00240264	The Real Blues Book	$34.99
00310910	The Real Bluegrass Book	$35.00
00240223	The Real Broadway Book	$35.00
00240440	The Trane Book	$22.99
00125426	The Real Country Book	$39.99
00269721	The Real Miles Davis Book C Edition	$24.99
00269723	The Real Miles Davis Book Bb Edition	$24.99
00240355	The Real Dixieland Book C Edition	$32.50
00294853	The Real Dixieland Book Eb Edition	$35.00
00122335	The Real Dixieland Book Bb Edition	$35.00
00240235	The Duke Ellington Real Book	$22.99
00240268	The Real Jazz Solos Book	$30.00
00240348	The Real Latin Book C Edition	$37.50
00127107	The Real Latin Book Bb Edition	$35.00
00120809	The Pat Metheny Real Book C Edition	$27.50
00252119	The Pat Metheny Real Book Bb Edition	$24.99
00240358	The Charlie Parker Real Book C Edition	$19.99
00275997	The Charlie Parker Real Book Eb Edition	$19.99
00118324	The Real Pop Book – Vol. 1	$35.00
00240331	The Bud Powell Real Book	$19.99
00240437	The Real R&B Book C Edition	$39.99
00276590	The Real R&B Book Bb Edition	$39.99
00240313	The Real Rock Book	$35.00
00240323	The Real Rock Book – Vol. 2	$35.00
00240359	The Real Tab Book	$32.50
00240317	The Real Worship Book	$29.99

THE REAL CHRISTMAS BOOK
00240306	C Edition	$32.50
00240345	Bb Edition	$32.50
00240346	Eb Edition	$35.00
00240347	Bass Clef Edition	$32.50
00240431	A-G CD Backing Tracks	$24.99
00240432	H-M CD Backing Tracks	$24.99
00240433	N-Y CD Backing Tracks	$24.99

THE REAL VOCAL BOOK
00240230	Volume 1 High Voice	$35.00
00240307	Volume 1 Low Voice	$35.00
00240231	Volume 2 High Voice	$35.00
00240308	Volume 2 Low Voice	$35.00
00240391	Volume 3 High Voice	$35.00
00240392	Volume 3 Low Voice	$35.00
00118318	Volume 4 High Voice	$35.00
00118319	Volume 4 Low Voice	$35.00

Complete song lists online at www.halleonard.com

Prices, content, and availability subject to change without notice.

0719
318

THE REAL BOOK MULTI-TRACKS

TODAY'S BEST WAY TO PRACTICE JAZZ!
Accurate, easy-to-read lead sheets and professional, customizable audio tracks accessed online for 10 songs

1. MAIDEN VOYAGE PLAY-ALONG
Autumn Leaves • Blue Bossa • Doxy • Footprints • Maiden Voyage • Now's the Time • On Green Dolphin Street • Satin Doll • Summertime • Tune Up.
00196616 Book with Online Media...........$17.99

2. MILES DAVIS PLAY-ALONG
Blue in Green • Boplicity (Be Bop Lives) • Four • Freddie Freeloader • Milestones • Nardis • Seven Steps to Heaven • So What • Solar • Walkin'.
00196798 Book with Online Media $17.99

3. ALL BLUES PLAY-ALONG
All Blues • Back at the Chicken Shack • Billie's Bounce (Bill's Bounce) • Birk's Works • Blues by Five • C-Jam Blues • Mr. P.C. • One for Daddy-O • Reunion Blues • Turnaround.
00196692 Book with Online Media $17.99

4. CHARLIE PARKER PLAY-ALONG
Anthropology • Blues for Alice • Confirmation • Donna Lee • K.C. Blues • Moose the Mooche • My Little Suede Shoes • Ornithology • Scrapple from the Apple • Yardbird Suite.
00196799 Book with Online Media $17.99

5. JAZZ FUNK PLAY-ALONG
Alligator Bogaloo • The Chicken • Cissy Strut • Cold Duck Time • Comin' Home Baby • Mercy, Mercy, Mercy • Put It Where You Want It • Sidewinder • Tom Cat • Watermelon Man.
00196728 Book with Online Media $17.99

6. SONNY ROLLINS PLAY-ALONG
Airegin • Blue Seven • Doxy • Duke of Iron • Oleo • Pent up House • St. Thomas • Sonnymoon for Two • Strode Rode • Tenor Madness.
00218264 Book with Online Media $17.99

7. THELONIOUS MONK PLAY-ALONG
Bemsha Swing • Blue Monk • Bright Mississippi • Green Chimneys • Monk's Dream • Reflections • Rhythm-a-ning • 'Round Midnight • Straight No Chaser • Ugly Beauty.
00232768 Book with Online Media $17.99

8. BEBOP ERA PLAY-ALONG
Au Privave • Boneology • Bouncing with Bud • Dexterity • Groovin' High • Half Nelson • In Walked Bud • Lady Bird • Move • Witches Pit.
00196728 Book with Online Media $17.99

9. CHRISTMAS CLASSICS PLAY-ALONG
Blue Christmas • Christmas Time Is Here • Frosty the Snow Man • Have Yourself a Merry Little Christmas • I'll Be Home for Christmas • My Favorite Things • Santa Claus Is Comin' to Town • Silver Bells • White Christmas • Winter Wonderland.
00236808 Book with Online Media..........$17.99

10. CHRISTMAS SONGS PLAY-ALONG
Away in a Manger • The First Noel • Go, Tell It on the Mountain • Hark! the Herald Angels Sing • Jingle Bells • Joy to the World • O Come, All Ye Faithful • O Holy Night • Up on the Housetop • We Wish You a Merry Christmas.
00236809 Book with Online Media..........$17.99

11. JOHN COLTRANE PLAY-ALONG
Blue Train (Blue Trane) • Central Park West • Cousin Mary • Giant Steps • Impressions • Lazy Bird • Moment's Notice • My Favorite Things • Naima (Niema) • Syeeda's Song Flute.
00275624 Book with Online Media $17.99

12. 1950S JAZZ PLAY-ALONG
Con Alma • Django • Doodlin' • In Your Own Sweet Way • Jeru • Jordu • Killer Joe • Lullaby of Birdland • Night Train • Waltz for Debby.
00275647 Book with Online Media $17.99

13. 1960S JAZZ PLAY-ALONG
Ceora • Dat Dere • Dolphin Dance • Equinox • Jeannine • Recorda Me • Stolen Moments • Tom Thumb • Up Jumped Spring • Windows.
00275651 Book with Online Media $17.99

14. 1970S JAZZ PLAY-ALONG
Birdland • Bolivia • Chameleon • 500 Miles High • Lucky Southern • Phase Dance • Red Baron • Red Clay • Spain • Sugar.
00275652 Book with Online Media $17.99

15. CHRISTMAS TUNES PLAY-ALONG
The Christmas Song (Chestnuts Roasting on an Open Fire) • Do You Hear What I Hear • Feliz Navidad • Here Comes Santa Claus (Right down Santa Claus Lane) • A Holly Jolly Christmas • Let It Snow! Let It Snow! Let It Snow! • The Little Drummer Boy • The Most Wonderful Time of the Year • Rudolph the Red-Nosed Reindeer • Sleigh Ride.
00278073 Book with Online Media $17.99

HAL•LEONARD®
www.halleonard.com